The Transition

Girl to Woman In and Out of Love

Featuring
How? Why? What! Who?
The Affair
&
When the Tables Turn
Poetry

By
Queen Seer

KATRINA'SWORKS
PUBLISHING LLC

ISBN: 13:978-0692890127

ISBN: 10:0692890122

The Transition

Girl to Woman In and Out of Love

Queen Seer

Copyright © June 2017

Cover Design

By

Katrina'sWorks Publishing LLC

Katrinasworks.com

Dedication

Dedicated to Dorothy L. Smith-Henderson

(Mommy)

Will someone wake me from this everlasting

dream that I dream

And it seems

That I would never find the meaning

On the signs

I see life as a book without meaning to it

And walk around in a daze without a high I sit

Hoping of making something

Out of nothing

With a pen and pad

Jotting down my happiness and sadness

~Queen Seer

Contents

Girl to Woman
In and Out of Love

Where are all the real young men?

~Written at fourteen

When I was fourteen just started dating
I would ask myself
Where are all the real young men?
Who stands there ground and know that I can
Once with me he knows the plan
When we talk don't ask me about sex
Could we go to the hotel and all that mess
I don't care if my shirt is short
And my blouse has my breast showing
You can say you'll take care of me forever
And I'm still not going
Who do you think I am? I not a Freak
Or a slut either giving my love
To any boy that pays attention to me
Calling me late at night like "Can we get together?"
I replied, "Not this late at night are you crazy?"
"Man forget you."
"Yeah... Whatever"

Where are all the real young men
Sweet romantic smooth... as they take you by the
hand
Looking into your eyes "Can I be your friend?"
Um..... Yea.... that's what I'm talking about
You other boys keep my name out of your mouth
And thoughts of me out of your mind
I look for a boy that's my kind
So where are all the real young men?
Stand up or raise your hand
Where are all the real young men?

Friends or Lovers

~Written at fifteen

Do I really have a friend?
The type that has my back and stick with me to the
end
Someone I can run and talk to when things don't go
my way
If I was sick in the hospital they'll come see me
everyday
And in relationships
Things are going wrong they have tips
To make things better
A friend stick with you whenever
And if your friend
Is a man
He knows what ground he stands
And never making other plans
If so he never was a friend
He was just another brother trying to get into things
You know what I mean "Open yo' legs you know we
friends"
And just like that you're right into it
When all alone you knew what he was doing
Then you want to look stupid
Once the relationship over and he is gone
Saying to your female friends "Girl, you know he
wrong."
But lovers are lovers
Friends are friends
Others are others
And that's the end.

Slow Dance

~ Written at sixteen

We're at the prom and as you take me to the
floor
My feelings for you grow strong and I'm not
afraid anymore
My arms resting on your shoulders
Remembering what I was told
When you ask me out
How you were shy
And, your hands covered your mouth
I knew what you would say so I said okay
That's why we're here today
Taking a chance
To find real romance
As we slow dance.

Dream of My Prince Charming

~Written at eighteen

My love I see that you have come at long last
And I have been waiting patiently for you
I have dreamed of this moment but it now in the
past
You are here with me as I gaze at you

We hold hands take walks through the park
You bring me flowers for no occasion
Am I in a fairytale?
Please tell me this man is for real
Or better yet don't tell me anything
Just let me keep imagining my prince charming

Now as I reemerge into the real world
And I look at the man that I care for
He's not charming at all

In fact he accuses me
Of doing things
That I wouldn't in my wildest dreams
And it seems

That I should be alone
Because I couldn't talk to him over the phone
For too long
Because I know that he would be gone

Within the hour
And it took all of my power
To stop from saying
I know that you are laying

With someone other than me
But, I know that we are not married

So instead of throwing stone for stone for stone
Or finding that backup plan to bone
I sit at home alone

Because unlike others I see no reason to be a
FREAK!!
Well..... Not for the moment

Or doing that hold up get off me
I think the condom broke could you stroke
Instead of poke
I hope that's not all you got

Wake up!! Are you sleep?
What about me?
Ahh... Please!!

Some of y'all know what I mean
So I go back to imaging
And hoping
My prince charming exist
And if not I can say this
I can dream.

Fairytale Land

~Written at eighteen

When I was a little girl
I was wrapped in my own world

I would be swept off my feet by this night and
shining armor
He would take me away always defending my
honor
Love me as I love him like a song
Love and be loved in return... I was wrong
I was told never judge a book by its cover
Because the one that you judge may just be your
lover
One way or another
It's like trying to run away with a puddle of oil
under your feet
You can't escape reality
Love isn't always discovered at first sight
Realism is far beyond Cinderella and Snow
White
I had to awake from fairytale land
Because while my back was turned
My love was flirting with a friend
And leading a secret life that I knew nothing
about
Once confronted he was in doubt
Lies, lies, and more lies
To make up for the lies
He told at first
Why didn't anyone warn me

That being in love sometimes hurts

Now that I'm an adult

As a result
I'm dealing with some real life shit
Men aren't always faithful
Willing to give any chick the dick
See some women are hoes
That may be true
Some men are dogs
Which category are you? I'm an adult as a result
I'm dealing with realty.

A Man Realizes He Loves a Woman

~Written at seventeen

Long walks in the park holding hands
Smooth touches soft kisses show romance
"Give me a chance
And I'll show you I'm your man." he said

"We're deeply involved
Without a cause
So where do we stand
This isn't how it was
I try to figure out how me and you became
an us"
She said

Others see it and they want it
We know it so we flaunt it
Don't it make you wonder....?

"Love is in the air cupid shot me cause I'm
falling for you
When push comes to shove
There's no limits to what I'll do for you.
I'm with you, and you with me
I'll be here for you whenever you need.
You are my queen."
"And, you are my king."

We're in love

Others see it and they want it
We know it so we flaunt it
Don't it me you wonder....

What love is
This is love.

For Closer

~Written at eighteen

Hey, what's up I remember you
See back in the day we were crazy cool
Had a car I think baby blue
But it wasn't brand new
You.....blew my mind each and every time
You'd come around
Call and say you were coming over
And I would be down
I was in love... I think
Because every time you'd come around
I'd get weak in the knees
Like SWV
My breathing would become slow
And in my mind I just didn't know
Was this meant to be
Or was I just blinded
By what my eyes couldn't see
Friends say that I had fell to deep
In a tunnel of love
To deep
For me
To see
Deceived, ignored, then belittle like a child
Once with you it was hard for me to smile
Wondering why was I with you for that while
But as we go our separate ways
Leave knowing you help me today
For closer.

Play the Fool

~ Written at eighteen

What do you want? Don't touch me
I don't want to hear it
You've done me wrong for the last time you
see
I have cried my last tear
Why did you apologize?

Then tell me you would change
Today I realized
That you will always be the same

How many times did I play the fool?
It's just the same old song
I would give my life to you
And you still managed to do me wrong
My legs would open wide to you
A well as my heart

You treated me like warned down shoes
You never loved me from the start
How many times did I play the fool?
I'm sorry I ran out of fingers to count
Five times I count you being rude

But you loved me five times less that
amount
Don't flatter me with your sick little lies
Telling me what you think I want to hear
Don't kiss me or try and rude my thighs
Put this car in the park gear
How many times did I play the fool?
I ignored the fact that you were unfaithful
As the signs stood in my face
I never once said I hated you

In fact I took you back with open arms
Let's leave the past behind
Maybe the third time will be a charm
This time everything will be fine
I played the fool for the last time
And that's how it's going to be
No more break up to make up lies
I have put my foot down you see
No more being a fool
I'm free at last
I have grown tired of you
Let's leave the past in the past
No more me and you.

Bitter Love

~Written at nineteen

We fuss and fight

Rant and rave

As we start digging early graves

No sweet hellos bitter goodbyes

Nights wrapped in hollow sighs

I yell and scream until no more

You turn then walk out the front door

No sweet hellos bitter goodbyes

Neither admits what love still lye

We say goodbye go separate ways

Eyes connect in an angry gaze

No sweet hellos bitter goodbyes

For we're in love but in denial.

Love Yourself

~Written at nineteen

Coming home from work she had a late
night
Soon as she step in the door her man want to
fight
Asking her where she been and who she been
with?
Then she replied, "Now I'm too tired to talk
about this..."
But, in a blink of an eye his hand raised to
the sky
Then after she replied
He had already blacked her eye
I tell you no lies
She cried
As he tried to explained
Three days later she asked her friend
What should she do?
Her friend replied

"Move...
Before he have your family singing the blues
Choose to be a winner not loser of your life
Because some grown ass man couldn't keep
his hands to himself
Alright,
No love is deeper than the love you have for
self

Keep depending on someone else
Prepare to get let down
This clown
Can't help you grow beating you to you black
and blue
Just thought you should know."

Before she had a chance to get away
She was at home the very next day
Going through the same thing now ain't that
a shame.

Be Careful What You Wish For

~Written a twenty

I wished upon a shooting star one day
Asking God to make my life okay
And, to take some of the stress away
In time it was granted
So now I having a few nice things
An automobile but no bling-bling
So I decided to ask for more
Lord send me a man that I adore
Someone who is attractive
And would love
To give me love

And in time it was granted

I meet a tall dark skinned handsome guy
Who wanted to give me the world
He stood right by side
At all times
Wiping the tears from my eyes
When I cry
And everyday
He would say
I love you
But...
This man had no realistic goals
Didn't want to work
And always stayed at home
We couldn't make it off love alone

So again I asked God

To send me a man with a car and a house
Who's responsible and knows what adulthood is
about

And would love to take me out

It was granted

I met a tall bright skinned responsible man
That did for me all that he can
His house and car was very nice
He wined and dined just right

Took me out me out every other night

But he gave me love
Only at a price.

Loving My Man

~Written at twenty- one

Hands wrapped around my waist
As we look face to face
Staring into each other's eyes
Surprise!!

I'm in love
Hoping that you are too
Because without me there is no you

Trusting you don't have any regrets
Remembering the first time that we met
I never knew a man
At first sight grab me by the hand
For life already making plans
Asking where do we stand?
Or could he be my man?

As I look at your lips
Thinking about how you grab my hips
Giving me tips
On how to better my life
Once with me he could make things right
If we get together
He'd banished my rainy weather

So he say
And in this case

I'm loving my man
My black man I'm Loving
Darker than the darkest night
Will I get with him?
Damn right!!!
I'd say it all day and night
Other men couldn't get this right

So if you ask me if my love is real
I'm loving my man that's the deal
Loving... my black man.

HOW? WHY? /WHAT! WHO?

The Affair

~Written at twenty one

The Wife

How dare you turn your back on me?
We have come so far, fine time to abandon
me now
Why do you want to hurt me? **How?**
After all that we have been through
Did I not love you enough?
How could you go behind my back with that
slut?

Why?
After all the years, emotion, and tears
The love that I invested in you
Did our marriage not mean
Anything!!
How? Why?

The Husband

What happened to the woman I fell in love
with?
It seem so long ago that we would kiss
I miss that, now all we do is fuss and fight
Who is this bitter woman I lay beside every
night?
What happen to the woman I fell in love

with?
Now you're asking me **why?** And **How?**
Well I'm tired of being unhappy.

The Wife

But, **why?** Does she make you happy?
Or, are you just tired of being in a
committed relationship?
Did you stop and think for a moment I'm
tired
Of being tied
Down too!!!
But, I loved you
When I said for better or worst I meant it
Even attempted to look over this affair
How could you? I guess you never cared.

The Husband

What!?!?
Temptation is what got me here
You don't do
The things you use to

The Wife

How could you put this all on me
I'm unhappy...

Too
But I didn't find
Time to creep
Or sleep
Around

The Husband

I'm sorry okay, just tell me **what** can I do
For you to give me another chance?
Forgive me
I still love you baby
What can I do?

The Wife
I don't know
We'll see
We will see.....

HOW? WHY? /WHAT! WHO?

When the Tables Turn

~Written at twenty one

The Husband

How could you?
Sleep with another man under my roof?
Why? What did you have to prove?
If I can do it so can you
A real mature thing to do
What I did was a mistake
You did this intentionally out of hate.

The Wife

When you cheated, were you thinking of my
feelings?
Oh, I guess it was just killing you
To lay between her legs every night
Only to do God knows **what** it's sick
Then come home and kiss me on the lips
Throwing our future away
So that you can say sorry later
But this doesn't make the pain go away
Does it? **Who** do you think you are?

The Husband

I'm only a man who made a mistake
How can I prove to you that it wasn't on
purpose?
You on the other hand intended to hurt me

I thought that you were better than that
Why?

The Wife

See I knew about your affair with her
I would lay in bed alone and there
I would think about you with your mistress
"The other woman"
While I'm left at home
Alone
Wondering
Where did I go wrong?
Then you would come home
And I would smell her perfume
In the back of my mind
Sometimes
I'd wish this would be you
What if the tables turned?
Could you take me being unfaithful?

The Husband

No I can't
But, **why** throw stone for stone?

The Wife

Well imagine **how** I felt
But I dealt
With it asking myself **why? How?**
I wanted you to understand **how I** you feel

The Husband

Well you spelled it out loud and clear

The Wife

So where do we go from here?

The Husband

I don't know
I really just don't know?

Get out

~Written at twenty one

You tremble and shake
As you await
The slashing of my tongue
A night of fun
Then you come home
And ask "What's going on?"
You know what's next
No need to fret
Take your punishment like a man
As I drove by
We connected eye to eye
While you and her were holding hands
No apology
Is really needed
This is the way life goes
So pack your shit!!
Then get out quick
Your cheating ass has got to go.

My Weekend

~Written at Twenty Two

Let me tell you of my romantic weekend
That never ended
How he expressed his feelings
Without telling me
With the food he prepared for me to eat
The bath water that smelled of peach
The way he rubbed my feet
While on his knees
Showed me
I was a Goddess in this man eyes
And at that moment I was at my weakest
point
Willing to surrender myself to him at his
command

The way he crawled into bed
Slowly kissing and caressing every inch of my
being
As if he read a book of my secret desires
And acted them out piece
He released unto me....passion
Quietly and as I tried to speak he "shushed"
then kissed me
And proceeded his journey of my body
This size 16 felt like a 10
Then he went in
Warm drenched body

He went in slowly
He went in and stayed until the next
morning
And as I crawled out of bed tingling
While attempting to caught my balance
Then tried to recollect what happened
I look at him he smiled
All the while
Not having to ask if I enjoyed my experience
While looking in the mirror
It was clear
This man had rocked my world
Yes!!!
My weekend never ended but extended.

You Are Real

~Written at twenty three

I take ten in a half steps
And what's left
I meet
Look up and see
The man of my dreams
Standing before me
And I am speechless...ly
Overwhelmed with happiness
My dark and gloomy day has turned to
daylight
What is it about you?
Could it be you looks
That took
Me away
To a place
Where I say
Your name with pride
Or possibly your words
Spoken oh so confidently
Makes me crave you like an addiction
What once was fiction
Is now reality
And you are real
My dream man is real.

Amazing Dark Skinned Woman

~Written at twenty-eight

You don't have to love me
Guess what I love myself
You don't have to see me truly in view of
You've chosen to see someone else
I didn't chose the skin that I'm in
Yet proudly I'm in it
Moreover in reality that's all that concerns
you
No matter how **DEEP** you think to be
You're just a classic black man
Yearning for a women with lighter skin
And that's alright
Though don't tell me, I'm the issue
Everybody has problem and complications
within themselves
Including you so be honest with yourself

The new lighter woman that you're
with... Huh she got issues too
But you choose to overlook them
Ironically funny
So wear her on your arms proudly
In light of you deserve what's appealing
Again for me it was my dark skin that was
your dilemma
My skin... my skin... my beautiful dark skin
that I'm in
You hated it
I embrace it
Now put that in your cigar paper and blaze
it
Sad that you didn't fully recognize that I'm
amazing
Along with that I loved you unconditional
with all your flaws
But most of all
I loved your dark skin.

The Other Woman

~Written at Twenty Four

I spend so much time staring at these four walls
And at night when I'm alone they call
Out to me
Love doesn't live here anymore just a vacancy
Maybe it was meant to be
Many nights spent in bedroom that belong to other
women
But it only took a minute to check out how I was
living
Foul
But in the meanwhile
I was destined to be alone
A mistress
Misfit
Miserable
The reflection in the mirror
Disappeared
This was not me
I wanted a man of my own
But I knew what I done
Would come back on me
So I will forever be lonely.

Grimy

~Written at Twenty Four

What once was grimy
Now spick and span clean
I worked my finger to the bone
To build a home for you and me
But all alone
You should've been a man
And stepped up to the plate
Supported you throughout the years
To change now would be too late
Once I gave you an ultimatum
I told you on that day
Either you step up to responsibility or walk away
My body grew tired
But soul willing and able
To keep pushing on
Alone
To reach my goals so everyday
I say
A prayer for you
I hope you doing well
Because so many years
And tears
Was spent with you living in hell
I'm doing swell here without you
There's no doubt that I can make it
I just look over my life
And think about all the abuse
That I have taken from you.

Lonely Heart

~Written at Thirty Two

Love is beautiful
But sometimes
Unreachable
Untouchable
So close but still unobtainable
To long for something you feel you can't have
So....so close yet can't grab
It's like insanity
Misery
A miserable feeling
That can't be contained
So what do you do about it?
Fake it to you make it or just feel blue about it?

Pray about it
Asking God to remove this bitter taste
For that sweet nectar love
That is dangled in front of you
Teasing you
Like child reaching for candy
Than at the last possible second
It's rip away
Mocking you
"Nah... Nah, Nee... Nah...
Nah...you...can't... caught...me..."

Oh but I will
Sooner or later I will
I will feel that

Heart beating
Pulse racing
Toe tingling
Overwhelming feeling
That comes from another person
That richer or poorer
Sickness and in health
Death do us part
Love…
There for me whenever I need
Love…
I will get it have it and hold it
One day
So keep playing taunting me love
Because one day I will be
In love deeply
Completely
One day.

Rose Painted Glasses

~Written at Thirty Two

If only you knew
How confused
Delusional
You sound as if sleep yet awake at the same
time
You think that you see things clearly
But you vision is blurred
I wish that you'd awake
And see the damage you done
In your belligerent state
But you want until you remove
Those rose painted glasses off your face
Because your past no matter
How far you travel to escape
Still places a role in your life today
What frames shall I get for you
I'll help you to remove those
Rose painted glasses
And replace them with bifocals
So that you may see things closer
Clearer
As they are
Instead of as you "think" that they appear
It's never easy to own up to your mistakes
So you place
These rose painted glasses on your face
Hoping that your past would somehow be

erased
Instead it stands
Stands before you
Waiting to reveal it's ugly truth

The day you stand
Stand in your truth as a man
Or woman
Will be the day
Those rose painted glasses
Would be lifted off your face
Then destroyed
And there in that moment
You will truly be free.

My Laughing Heart

~Written at thirty two

Once upon a time
We had a conversation
Randomly
Then later passed each other on the by
Seldomly
Saw each other
Smile and wave
Then all of a sudden
We gazed
Into each other's eyes
I waited on you
Speak to me
Thinking
Dear God please don't let him be crazy
And for heaven sake let him have a brain
Later becoming the best of friends
Snuggling on the couch
I'd wish this feeling would never end
I'd never laugh so much
Or felt so safe
Today....
Is your wedding day
And to my dear friend I wish you
All the happiness you deserve
I smile but hate it had to be with her.

Dedicated to MLH

A Gem

~Written at thirty two

You stand before me
As if you want to say something
But, before you speak
I need you to see
See me as the gem
That I am

Call me...
A Centenary Diamond
Or because I am rare call me
Darya-ye Noor Diamond
Open your eyes wide and peep this beautiful
magnificent jewel
That is before you
And before you speak
Just know I am flux
Within my own right

Though not flexible so you cannot change
me
I am winsomeness beauty at its rarest form
I hope you see it

Or if cataracts run in your family
You can just listen

Listen to the sound of my voice
And though I am not forced
To choose my words wisely
I do so respectably

I hope you are like a jeweler
That recognizes something valuable
Exquisite when it is upon you
Because like a once in a lifetime opportunity
If I leave.... I'm unlikely to return
So I advise thy choose your words wisely
Now speak to me.

Ms. S.H.I.T

~Written at twenty-six

I'm the S.H.I.T tell yo' friends about me
Been with all shades
From dark brown to pale pink
And they all say I'm fly
I keep 'em coming no lie
When the doors closed
Thought I was supposed
To make a grown man cry
From my head to my feet
Couldn't tell that I'm a freak
I wear long jeans and sleeves
I'm such a F***ing Lady
Some don't know
About me misbehaving
Other than the many men
That's been in my den
Saying you're the shit baby

I'm a Sexy Hot Intensive Teaser(SHIT)
They'd say please I really need ya
I'd say nah'll bae as if I'd been deceiving them
They say I'm evil or just mean
But they can't see

That it's just me
And it's the way it's gotta be
Cause they'd get angry I do admit
Cause they'd ask again and with a grind
I'd say "Do you have a condom?" They'd say SHIT!!!

Freaky Thoughts

~Written at twenty-six

You're a tall dark sexy man
(In my mind)
I'm like "Come and get up on it"
I walk slow pass him show him how I flaunt it
If you want it come and get it
Show me that you want it
Don't be scared, hop up on it

(Now in reality)
The conversation going real well
Man I think you're fine

(In my mind)
So let me spit this game to you baby
Try and blow your mind
You'll never find a chick like me
I'm one of a kind
I'm feeling good
You lookin right
So can we do this thing tonight?

(Now in reality)

When you kissed me
Softly
My mind went blank
Now I'm physically attracted to your mind

Not your bankroll
Hoes fall a dime a dozen
Real women stand in truth
And I would be lying
If I say I wasn't feeling you

(In my mind)
I know you want me
I can see it in your eyes
So when I rip your clothes off
Don't try and act surprise
I'll take control and start it first
And you end it as if rehearsed
And if I'm cursed
To make you burst first
Then let me end it with a really big bang
Cause damn you know you fine
We've been digging each other for a while
Now I think it's time
Good things come to those who wait
And baby you've been patient
Now I love the way we having sexual
relation.

Miss Submissive

~Written at twenty-five

Come on in baby
I could see you had a hard day
So sit back
Relax
Tell me how I can take that stress away
Could I run a bath?
Or let you take a shower for an hour
While you decide what pleasures you desire
See I'm not hot I'm on fire
Burning with warm desire
see you high
But I'm about to take you
Higher
Lay on your stomach

Like that
While I rub oil on your back
kiss your neck
Let you unwind....
Before you start to sweat
Now tell me are you feeling this
The softness
Of my kiss
This
Ambition
Of bliss
I'm feeling with you

What we have is real
Love the way you make me feel
So be silent
Be still
While... I... Express my gratitude to you
While.... I .... Express my gratitude to you
While.... I .... Express my gratitude to you
I submit because I love you.

I Can't Play Me!!

~Written at twenty-four

3 Weeks ago
So I put my man out the other day
Low down cheating dog wanna play....me
So I packed his crap threw it on the curb
Freaking jerk got what he deserved
I told him "You can't play me, you no longer
can hurt me"

2 Weeks later
But when he apologized
I realized
I can't live
Without the love he gives
What we have is real

A Week ago
Real pathetic
Can't believe
He played me
I said that I wouldn't do this again
So I told him "You won't play me, never
again, you no longer can hurt me"

Today
So I peep this woman staring
I looked back cause she was just eyeing me
She shook her head and said
"Now, I know you can't be that dumb Queen"
So I told my *reflection*
"Hey!!! You can't play me you no longer can
hurt me!!"

THE TRANSITION

Inspection of Truth

Depend on the Lord

~Written at 12 years old

I was born with brown skin

So what that's not a sin

You may try and hurt me with your words

Push me aside and pretend that I'm not

heard

Call me out my name and expect me to be a

shame

I know I'm supposed to love my enemies

Even though that may be hard to do

For all the hurt pain and misery they put me

through

Turn the other cheek be strong not weak

Though your enemies may try and bring you

down

The Lord will always be around

And for all the hurt people put on you

Depend on the Lord and he'll see you

through.

Will I Be

~Written at 14 years old

Will I be a single black female?

Waiting to exhale

Trying to find me a distinguished gentlemen

With a job and benefits

Will I be a menace to society?

Getting high on Sugar Hill

Naw....That ain't the deal

Hot from the delta heat

Big stomach bare feet

Married with children as we live

All the days of our lives

Until we see our guiding light

Knowing now it's a different world

But I'm only a girl

Young and restless

Trying to give a message

I don't know where I would be in ten years

Happy may have shed tears

People may have tried to put me down

But in the other life I'll wear the crown

Having brought the Lord God with me

My destination I will see.

I Can Make It with God

~Written at 15 years old

As I look over my life and think about all the

things I have taken

Sometimes a question comes up can I really

make it

Staring right through the eyes of Satan

All odds against me as I'm shaking

Step aside because I will survive

God is on my side

Holding my hand

Taking me through my problems as only he

can

That's why I'm loving no man

Not as I love God that's the plan

You wonder when you talk about me, why do

I just take it?

Because I know with God I can make

When laughter surrounds me pointing its

finger

Because of my physical problems

I still stand strong

I know with God I can solve them

I can make it

Whatever life throws at me I can shake it

Because against all odds

I can make with God

My Room

~Written at 15 years old

Where do I go to hide?

When life seem so hard I cannot strive?

Where do my deepest innermost secrets lie?

Or the first place I cried

When someone if my family died?

To my room

Where do I go to escape?

The pain I face

Day to day

To let my mind be free

And focus more on me?

To my room.

Ms. Lose It

~Written at 16 years old

I can lose almost anything
From a sheet of paper to a diamond ring
I'm unmatched

Often told I can lose my head if it wasn't
attached

You may give me something for years to
keep

Weather sour or sweet
With me

It'll be gone within a week
Lost and can't be found
So people say I'm low down
I tell them stick around

I once was lost but now I'm found
I can lose almost anything
To me there's nothing to it
You might as well call me

Ms. Lose it.

Mama Don't Wipe Away My Tears

~Written at 17 years old

Mama at times I come to you with tears in my
eyes
Life has taken its toile on me that's why I cry
Mama no
Don't wipe away my tears let them show
I'll be fine this is how I grow

Don't you try and make things better
One day sunshine will clear up this stormy
weather
You taught me to be strong
Keep God in my life
Put him first
And everything will go right
I love you mama
But don't wipe away my tears
I'll be fine.

I am Beautiful

~ Written at 17 years old

I would wonder what men see in me

Is it my looks or just my individuality?

Or is it the short skirts

That make them hurt when I walk by?

Or the shyness

Because they never saw much of my eyes

Was it my curves?

Or the swirl in my walk

The soft way that I talk

It takes a special man to see me truly

I am beautiful

It took a long time for me to say those

words

In regards to myself

I've been knocked down

Thrown around

And left alone with a frown

But with my scars and bruises

I stand before you today

And say

I am beautiful.

Oh Little Girl

~Written at 17 years old

Oh, little girl

That think that she is grown

Stop and listen so I can tell you what's going on

Stepping out of the house with your butt and chest

showing

Not listening because you do not think it's wrong

Oh little girl

Laid all out in the bed

Some man told you, you were pretty

You let it go to your head

Lied about your age

Now you are afraid

Little do you know?

You could be laid

In an ally dead

Oh little girl

Times get hard doesn't

Now you transformed into a woman

But, your childhood years was better wasn't it
Wishing you were grown when you were a child
Now a woman wishing you can turn back the hands
of time

Oh, little girl
You unknowingly took on a role you couldn't handle
Disrespecting your parents saying without them you
could manage
Sleeping with multiple men
Hoping one day to process a ring on your hand

Oh, little girl
Wipe the tears from your eyes
While you rock a by your babies to stop them from
crying
It will get better just keep living
Put trust in God
Because love he's forever giving

Oh, little girl
I know you think to yourself you made a mistake
You feel as though you dreaming but when will you
awake

This is reality there is no escape
You have made your bed now you must lay

Oh little girl
So lost and used

Oh little girl
So confused and misused

Oh little girl
So....so confused
Let me tell you what you should do
Depend on the lord and he'll see you through.

America 911

~Written at 17 years old

The death of many loved ones

Has shattered our dreams for lies ahead

We must be strong though many are gone

Our dreams must not be dead

Listen to the wise words

Let them not go down in vein

We as Americans should stand tall never be

ashamed

We go down in history for many battles won

But, the war is not yet over for many battles

won

But, the war is not yet over for it has just

begun

Keep your heads held high

Keep God right by your side

America will be strong and if God's will

We will not die.

Be Free

~Written at 17 years old

Long lost world, hidden behind lies and

deception

Come out and be free of all sin

Take the hand of religious faith

For heaven sake

Be free

The end of the world may be near

Closer than the mid could ever wander

Jesus is coming though many are not

ready to be judged

It seems that more people are dying

When it comes to telling the truth more

are lying

There's much depression so more are

sighing

We have lost sight

For what's right

So more are blind

When will this cycle ever end?

Seems like it's over when it's only just

beginning.

The Everlasting

~Written at 18 years old

When everything around me seems to

crumble up and fold

I take a deep breath and look around me

behold

There is still beauty

And I take time to thank God

I know I am not alone

And as the stars grace us once more

So deep and everlasting

At that moment I know he is still here

I'm never alone

Even if the whole world turned against me

Cutting me with their eyes

As to seem to be forever

With God's love and the strength of my spirit

I would smile

As if I disappeared in a mist of glory

There are reasons

That the seasons

Change

As well as the mood of all human beings

Though I may change

God's love for us will remain.

Subject without a Name

~ *Written at 18 years old*

Different skin colors other struggles made in this life
So I put fear aside so I can rise above all this... I
Feel like I'm trapped will I adapted or be lead astray
Is what I'm feeling inside a feeling I can obtain
It's strange almost insane how the world operate
Do I give up just out of luck or do I participate
Does anyone relate or understand what I have to say
Or am I just speaking on a subject without a name
Blame you ever you want for what happens to you
But in the end you just like me trapped without a
clue
Nowhere to run nowhere to hide nowhere left to
survive
So don't just fall to your knees and cry
Put God in your life to live, fight and pray
Just hope on judgment day God would open the
gate.

Truly

~Written at 18 years old

Break away from the normal
And there you would see yourself
Truly
We often mask ourselves
From what is truly our identity?
Hide in shells of what we consider normal
Only to hide ourselves
From others
Who are experiencing the same feelings?
Be not afraid to show yourself
Truly.

Angel

~Written at 18 years old

Awaken from complications and injuries

Only to see

Those big brown beautiful eyes staring back

at me

Wondering

Where will I be without her?

She was able to stop these four walls from

disappearing

Years spent listening to the knowledge she

put in my ear

She's now the voice inside my head pushing

me to continue on

My support system my backbone

If I were to gain success

I would be so bless

To take some stress

Out of her life

She provided for me

With swollen feet

As I would sleep at night

And I could be so lucky

Blessed with a mother so loving

You have touched me more than you could

ever know

Now as I get older

And the world becomes colder

I hope I always have that shoulder to lean

on

As I complain about my life and express to

you my anger

I still thank God

He has blessed me with an angel.

Giving Birth to Knowledge

~Written at 19 years old

When I speak

I want to reach

Touch you without lifting a finger

Linger

Circling within your inner thoughts

Without knowing

Growing

Even when you're away

My words would remain

Taking a form

You would hold

Within you

Allowing you to feed it more

Let it be my voice

The informs you of what's right

Let it be my voice that tucks you in at night

Then when time's up

Release what I have giving you unto the

world

Teach

Preach

Just be

An image of me.

Childlike Woman

~Written at 19 years old

Hear me

I allow you to enter me

Mentally

Fearlessly

Breaking rules instilled in permanent ink

That could never be torn but linked back to

me

You take away

The marks on my childlike face

Then say that I'm a baby

That's crazy

Is the years suddenly put away

Then I speak you know then I am a woman

I am a woman for a moment

I am a woman who have left here and came

back again

Silent

Yet I scream and dance with no movement

In tuned

Trying to adapt to a world

That doesn't yet know I exist

Mystify

All those around me

Who could care less if I am here?

Nor there

But for a moment I am somebody

I am a woman for a moment

Tomorrow arrives today

Then I say again

I am a woman

I dance and scream with no movement

In tune

Expressing my womanhood

With nothing to prove

But my non- innocents.

My Father

~Written at 15 years old

My father lives behind bars

Scared by society

Raising me to be his opposite

All the while

He's expiring me

Smiling constantly

Bluntly expressing his feeling

Giving me complete inspiration

I watched a drunk man fall to the floor as a

child

The same man lifted me up and tossed the

beer bottles to the side

Now he provides for his family

Teaching me what a real man

Should be god works mysteriously

Thank you lord for these blessing

But, behind bars he remain

And it's a shame

How life play such cruel games

And as I continue living

Giving bits and pieces to others

What was taught to me by him?

It's only clear

My father taught me

Life.

Dedicated to Alfred Lee Henderson

For the Man That Stands

~Written at 17 years old

Much respect

For those you caught

The B.U.S

To get

To their

J.O.B

Striving to survive

World cease

To let them be

Some push forward

To get forced back

While other just give up

Accepting misfortunes just as blessings

Another benefits off luck

In some cases you see their faces

As we're slowly cruising by

Each has a tale to tell

In which we never would reply

"An empire of riches could crumble to the ground
But for the man that stands at the bus stop
It doesn't make a sound."

That Evening

~Written at 19 years old

At times

When I wake up in the morning

Got to face the fact the you're gone

No more stories

No more lessons of history

Miss hearing your voice over the telephone

Seeing that chair

Where you would sit

Brings back so many memories

I still see your face

And the silly way

You use to smile

Every time

You look at me

It's funny how life works out

God knew that soon you were leaving

Now I cherish that moment

That we spent in the hospital room

That evening.

Dedicated to my Grandma (Lil Mama)

Minnie Mae Ealy

Simply Mommy

~Written at 32 years old

Listen to me speak, understand my words

I don't want to yell

But listen to me when I tell

You what's best for you, I mean well

Don't enough me

Don't even think of shunning me off

I'm trying to help

Don't think of yourself

How can I rescue one?

Who only knows how to be lost?

I want to save him

So I pray for him

Then inform him to behave

My son you will never be a slave

To this system

You are unprecedented

Represented

By the best

Me

Your mommy

And I will always love you.

Dedicated to my son Zerrion Fair

My Prayer

~Written at 31 years old

I've been stagnant for so long

I forgot how it feels to move

Been stuck in this rut

That it has altered my mood

I look at my reflection

And no longer recognize the face

Looking back at me

Please!!!

Lord Jesus hear my plea

Somewhere along this journey

I lost myself

I cry when I'm happy

Smile when I am not sad

I'm on my knees

Because on this day

I give it all to you Lord

Whatever I'm doing wrong

I pray that you reveal it to me

I give it all to you

I repent of my sins

Hold my hand

Lead me to me

So that I may feel whole again

This I ask in your son Jesus name

Amen.

Congratulations on the Marriage

~Written at 31 years old

This relationship has stood the test of time

As true love is endless and always forgiving

No matter what life throws your way

You two will always have each other

Not many get the chance say that

Many don't get the chance to experience true

love

So that is a gift within itself

I am proud of you both

For being great honest individuals

As well as an even better couple

May your lives be blessed

Because you both deserve it

I love you both.

(Dedicated to Tumira and Danny Brooks)

I Can Dream

~Written at 25 years old

I went from writing poetry

to writing out bills

I live

And work hard and was told the stress kills

Money rules the nation so work hard and just

chill

But I should have

Focused more on an education

So this emptiness could be filled

Now I just work to pay bills

Some say I'm dreaming my life away

Cause in my mind I'm the greatest

But others around me don't feel the same

At twenty five (25) I was alive just to be

kicking

Salt of the earth survive just to be giving

But in my mind

I could climb the highest mountains

In reality I'm afraid of heights

In my mind I love bright days

In reality I prefer nights

I could chit chat with the best of them

When really I'm too shy

In my mind I'm the richest woman on this

earth

In reality I'm just getting by

This world could consume everything

Robbed of all emotions and material things

But never will it ever take my ability to

dream.

My Externship

~Written at 32 years old

I'm shaking in my boots

The time morning 7:32

First day of extern

Yet don't know what to do

My nerves got the best of me

Feeling like I just turned 17

Yet and still I'm 33

And it's becoming hard to shake this feeling

Like everybody's watching me

I came to far to give up

Failing is not an option

Though it seems everything's going wrong

I know I could never stop

I must succeed attitude I will do

Lord grant me the strength

Rid my nerves so I may get through

My Externship

Inspection of Truth

~Written at 33 years old

The search for truth

It's as if seeking a needle in a haystack

Once on the trail of truth's existence

It's possible to run into setbacks

Then become sidetrack

By the many distractions

That holds your attention

Not to mention

The third dimension

High definition

Centuries of brainwashing

So become centered

Then embrace silence

Drawing power from within

Soul searching while knees bent

Pay close attention to what surrounds you

Open your eyes wide........ Inspections

Then once truth is found spread it

Consistently

Even if you think that no one is listening

Eventually

They'll get it

Truth.

About Queen Seer

I never really considered myself a writer, though it's been my dream for years. Poetry throughout my life was my way to vent; and with *Girl to Woman in and Out of Love,* it was my little secret. Penning *The Transition* I didn't have to conform myself to this little box called writing. With my poetry, I can be as constricted or as loose as I like...free to be myself. The *Inspection of Truth* I dedicate to my mother Dorothy L. Smith-Henderson who would tell me to do something with my poetry. She was my biggest fan.

RIH Mommy, Love You!

Connect with Queen Seer on Facebook

&

https://katrinasworks.com/authors/queen-seer/